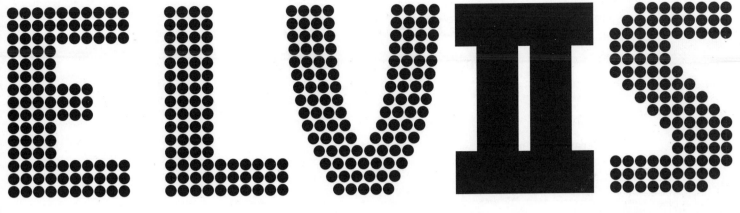

2ND TO NONE

Exclusive distributors:
Music Sales Limited
8/9 Frith Street, London W1D 3JB, England.
Music Sales Pty Limited
120 Rothschild Avenue, Rosebery, NSW 2018, Australia.

Order No. AM84666
ISBN 0-7119-2638-7
This book © Copyright 2003 by Wise Publications.

Music arrangements by Derek Jones.
Music processed by Paul Ewers Music Design.

Unauthorised reproduction of any part of this
publication by any means including photocopying
is an infringement of copyright.

Printed in the United Kingdom by
Caligraving Limited, Thetford, Norfolk.

www.musicsales.com

Your Guarantee of Quality:

As publishers, we strive to produce every book
to the highest commercial standards.

While endeavouring to retain the original running
order of the recorded album, the book has been carefully
designed to minimise awkward page turns and
to make playing from it a real pleasure.

Particular care has been given to specifying
acid-free, neutral-sized paper made from pulps which
have not been elemental chlorine bleached.

This pulp is from farmed sustainable forests and
was produced with special regard for the environment.

Throughout, the printing and binding have been
planned to ensure a sturdy, attractive publication
which should give years of enjoyment.

If your copy fails to meet our high standards,
please inform us and we will gladly replace it.

This publication is not authorised for sale
in the United States of America and/or Canada

Wise Publications
part of The Music Sales Group
London/New York/Paris/Sydney/Copenhagen/Berlin/Madrid/Tokyo

that's all right

Words & Music by Arthur Crudup

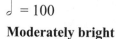

Moderately bright

Verse 4:

I'm leavin' town tomorrow, leavin' town for sure.
Then you won't be bothered with me hangin' 'round your door.
But that's all right, that's all right.
That's all right Mama, any way you do.

Verse 5:

Vocal ad. lib.
But that's all right, that's all right.
That's all right Mama, any way you do.

i forgot to remember to forget

Words & Music by Stanley Kessler & Charlie Feathers

time. _____ The day she went a - way I made my-self a
there. _____

prom-ise That I'd soon for - get we ev - er met. _____ But

some-thing sure is wrong 'cause I'm so blue and lone-ly. I for - got to re-

mem-ber to for - get. _____ When I'm get. _____

1. F   Bb7   F   2. F   Bb7   F

(Tacet)

blue suede shoes

Words & Music by Carl Lee Perkins

shoes.

You can do a - ny - thing_ but lay

off of my blue suede shoes._

Well, you can

knock me down,_ step on my face,_ slan - der my name all
burn my house,_ steal_ my car,_ drink_ my ci - der from my

ov - er the place;_ }
old_ fruit jar;_ }

Do a - ny - thing that you want to do,_ but

love me

Words & Music by Jerry Leiber & Mike Stoller

Treat me like a fool, treat me mean and cruel, but love me. Break my faith-ful heart, tear it all a-

your heart_____ beat - ing close to

mine._____ If you ev - er go, darl - ing I'll__ be oh, so

lone - ly,_____ beg - ging on my knees, all I ask is please,____ please

love me._____ I would beg and

i want you, i need you, i love you

Words by Maurice Mysels
Music by Ira Kosloff

mean woman blues

Words & Music by Claude DeMetrius

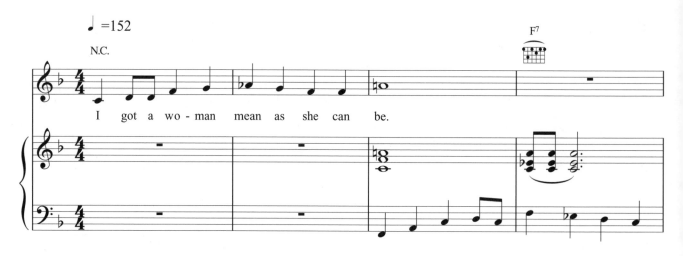

loving you

Words & Music by Jerry Leiber & Mike Stoller

where I go or what I do,

you know that I'll al - ways be lov - ing

you. If I'm seen with some - one new,

don't be blue, _ don't be blue. _ I'll be faith - ful

I'll be true; al - ways true,__ true to you.__

There is on - ly one for me, and you know

who. You know that I'll al - ways be

lov - ing you. lov - ing you.

rall.

king creole

Words & Music by Jerry Leiber & Mike Stoller

tar   with   a   great   big   soul._____   He
song   a - bout   a   jel -   ly   roll._____   He
plays   you   got   to   get   up   on   your   feet.   When   he

lays   down   a   beat   like   a   ton   of   coal,_____   He
starts   to   growl   from   way   down   in   his   throat._____   He
sings   a   song   a - bout   pork   and   greens._____   He
gets   the   rock - in'   fe - ver,   ba - by,   hea - ven   sakes,_____   He

N.C.

goes   by   the   name   of_____   King   Cre - ole.
bends   a   string   and   "That's_____   all   she   wrote."   } You   know   he's
sings   some   blues   a - bout_____   New   Or - leans.
don't   stop   play - in'   till   the   gui - tar   breaks.

B♭7

gone,   gone,   gone,   jump - in'   like   a

20

catfish on a pole._____

You know he's gone, gone, gone,

hip-shaking King Creole._____

1, 2, 3.

4.

2. When the
3. Well, he
4. Well, he

treat me nice

Words & Music by Jerry Leiber & Mike Stoller

fin - gers   through   my   hair._____   You

know   I'll   be   your slave_____   if   you   ask   me   to.___

___   But   if   you   don't   be- have,_____   I'll

walk   right   out   on   you.___   If   you   want   my   love   then   take___

24

wear my ring around your neck

Words & Music by Bert Carroll & Russell Moody

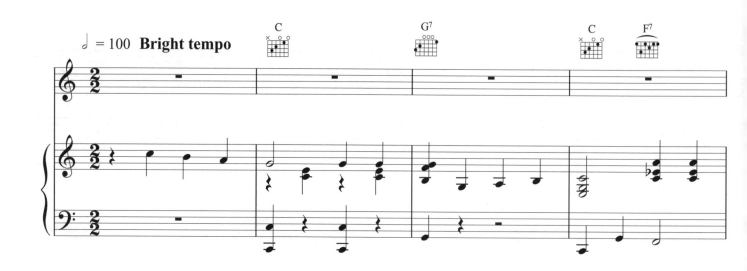

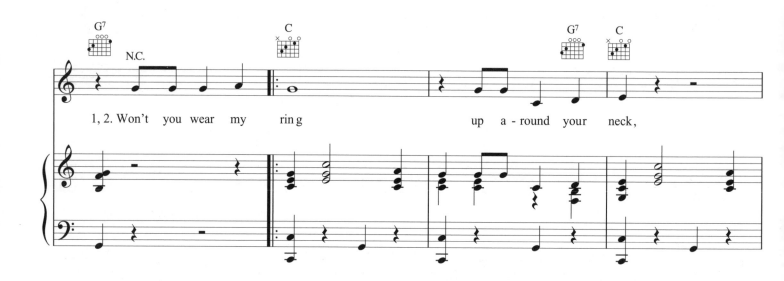

1, 2. Won't you wear my ring up a-round your neck,

to tell the world I'm yours, by heck.

Let them see your love for me,

— and let them see by the ring a - round your neck.

(2.)Won't you wear my neck.

They say that go - ing

stead - y is not the prop - er thing.

They say that we're too

young to know the mean-ing of a ring. I on-ly know I

love, love you and that you love me too. So, darl-ing, please do

what I ask of you. Won't you wear my ring

a-round your neck, to tell the world,

I'm yours, by heck.
Let them see / Let them know your love for / I love you

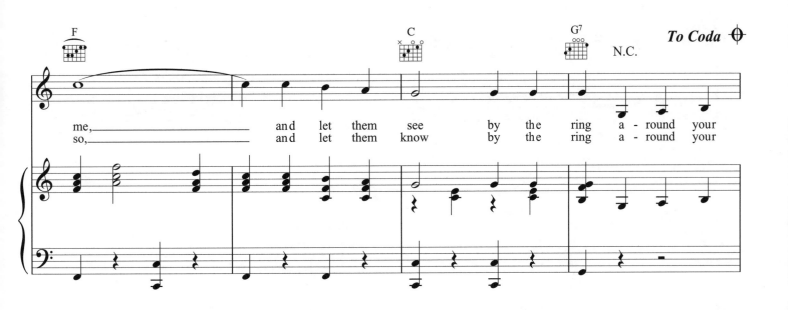

me,_____ and let them see by the ring a - round your
so,_____ and let them know by the ring a - round your

To Coda ⊕

N.C.

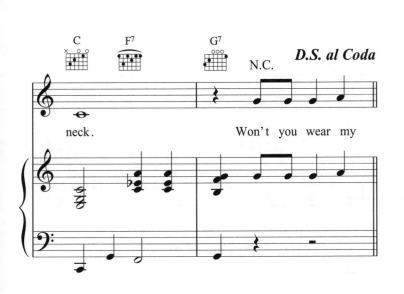

neck. Won't you wear my

D.S. al Coda N.C.

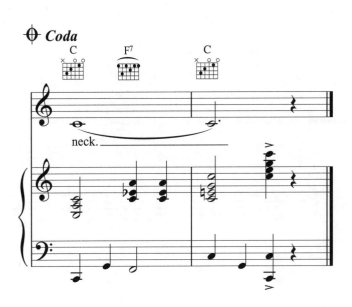

⊕ **Coda**

neck._____

trouble

Words & Music by Jerry Leiber & Mike Stoller

Slowly and Menacingly

1. If you're look-in' for trou-ble, you came to the right place.

If you're look-in' for trou-ble, just look right in my face.

I was born stand-ing up and talk-in' back.

2. I never looked for trouble but I never ran.
   I don't take no orders from no kind of man.
   I'm only made out of flesh, blood, and bone,
   But if you're gonna start a rumble, don't you try it all alone,
   'Cause I'm evil; my middle name is Misery.
   Yes, I'm evil, so don't you mess around with me.

i got stung

Words & Music by Aaron Schroeder & David Hill

Ho - ly smoke,_ a - land sakes a - live! I nev - er thought this could hap - pen to me._

Ah._____ Yeah! Ah._____

you. I'll be buzz - in' 'round your hive ev-'ry day at five, and I'm

nev - er gon - na leave____ once I ar - rive 'cause I'm

done, uh - huh, I got stung!

1.

2.

Ah,____ stung!____

i need your love tonight

Words & Music by Sid Wayne & Bix Reichner

need your love to-night.__ I've been wait-in' just for to-night to do some lov-in' and

hold you tight. Don't tell me, ba-by, you got-ta go;__ I got the hi-fi high and the

lights down low. Hey, now, hear what I say.__ Ooh-wow, you bet-ter stay.__ Pow-

pow, don't run a-way.__ I need your love to-night.__ Oh,__

a mess of blues

Words & Music by Doc Pomus & Mort Shuman

39

i feel so bad

Words & Music by Chuck Willis

Feel so __ bad, _____ feel like a ball- -game on a rain-y day. __

Feel so ___ bad, _____ feel like a ball-
- game on a rain-y day. _____

that's the way I feel._____
gain, I want to leave._____

Bb7

Oo._____
'Times I want to

leave here,__
then a - gain, I want to

Peo - ple, that's the way I
then a - gain, I want to

F7

feel._____
stay._____

44

little sister

Words & Music by Doc Pomus & Mort Shuman

ter.
tails.
ter,

Oh,   I   took   her   to   the   show.
Hey,   girl,   I   pinch   your   turned   up   nose.
Lord,   she's   with   some -   bo -   dy   new.

—
—
—

Hey,   I   went   for   some   can -   dy,   a   long
Aw,   but   ba -   by,   you've   been   grow -   in'   and   late la-
Aw,   she's   mean   and   she's   e -   vil   like   a

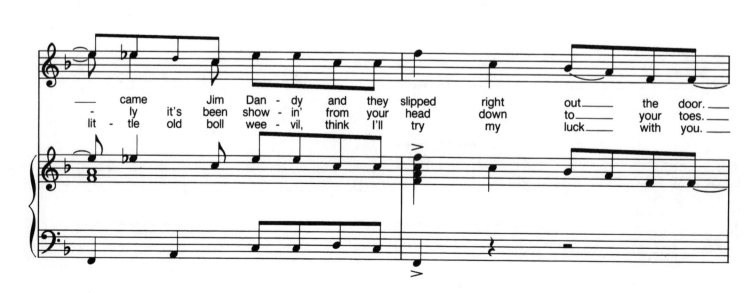

—   came   it's   Jim   Dan -   dy   and   they   slipped   right   out   the   door.
- ly   it's   been   show - in'   from   your   head   down   to   your   toes.
lit - tle   old   boll   wee - vil,   think   I'll   try   my   luck   with   you.

49

bossa nova baby

Words & Music by Jerry Leiber & Mike Stoller

"Take it ea - sy, baby, I worked all day and my feet feel just like lead.
"Hey, lit - tle ma - ma, let's sit down, have a drink and dig the band."
"Come on, baby, it's hot in here, and it's oh, so cool out - side.

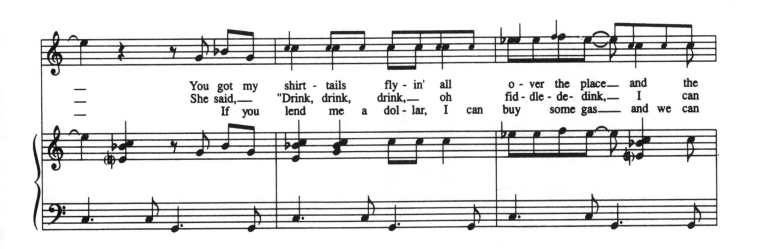

You got my shirt - tails fly - in' all o - ver the place and the
She said, "Drink, drink, drink, oh fid - dle - de - dink, I can
If you lend me a dol - lar, I can buy some gas and we can

53

rock-a-hula baby

Words & Music by Fred Wise, Ben Weisman & Dolores Fuller

55

viva las vegas

Words & Music by Doc Pomus & Mort Shuman

1.Bright light ci - ty gon - na set my soul___ gon - na set my
2.How I wish that___ there were more___ than the twen - ty four

soul on the fire.___ Got a whole lot of mo - ney that's___
hours in the day.___ 'Cause e - ven if there were___

58

night time, turn - in' night in - to day - time, if you see it once____ you'll

ne - ver be the same____ a - gain____

3. I'm gon - na keep on the run, I'm gon - na have me some fun if it

costs me my ve - ry last____ dime.____ If I wind up broke____

well I'll al-ways re-mem-ber that I had a swing-in' time.

I'm gon-na give it ev-'ry-thing I've got

La-dy Luck please let the dice stay hot. Let me shoot a se-ven with

ev-'ry shot. Vi-va Las Ve-gas,

if i can dream

Words & Music by W. Earl Brown

why,___ oh___ why,___ oh___ why___ can't my dream come true,_____ Oh___

why?_____ There must be peace and un - der - stand - ing_____

some - time,_____ Strong winds of prom-ise_____ that will blow a - way___ the

doubt_____ and fear; If I can dream_____ of a warm-er sun,___ Where

can - dle,___ And while I can think!___ While I can talk! While I can

stand!___ While I can walk! While I can dream _____ Please let my

dream _____ come true _____ right

now! _____

memories

Words & Music by Billy Strange & Mac Davis

don't cry daddy

Words & Music by Mac Davis

Dad-dy, Dad-dy, please laugh a-gain,_ Dad-dy, ride_ us on your back a-gain,_ Oh,

Dad — dy, please don't cry.

Oh, Dad — dy, please don't cry.____

kentucky rain

Words & Music by Dick Heard & Eddie Rabbitt

74

you don't have to say you love me

Words & Music by Vicki Wickham, Simon Napier-Bell,
Giuseppe Donaggio, Marino Atria & Vito Pallavicini

always on my mind

Words & Music by Wayne Thompson, Mark James & Johnny Christopher

82

an american trilogy

Traditional, arranged by Mickey Newbury

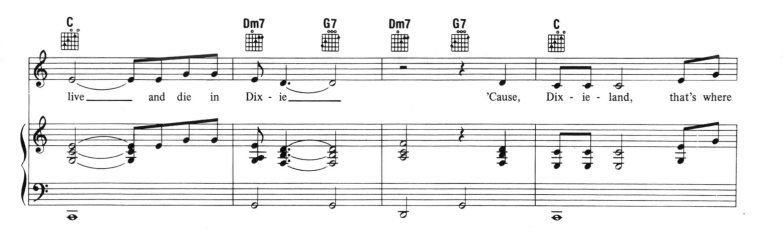

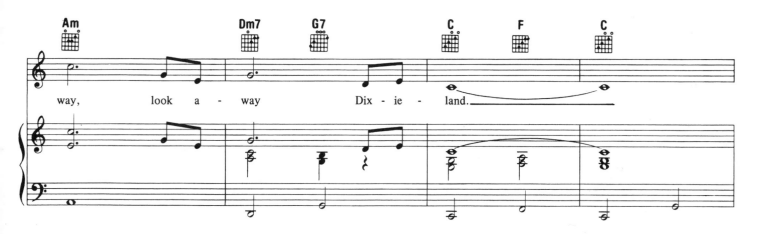

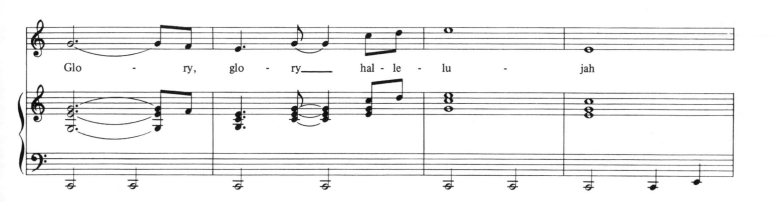

promised land

Words & Music by Chuck Berry

I left my home in Nor - folk, Vir - gin - ia, Ca - li - for - nia on my

mind,_____ I strad - dled that Grey - hound and rode___ him in - to Ral - eigh and on___

Verse 2:

Right away I bought me a through train ticket,
Ridin' across Mississippi clean,
And I was on the Midnight Flyer out of Birmingham,
Smokin' into New Orleans.
Somebody helped me get out of Louisiana,
Just to help me get to Houston Town.
There are people there who care a little about me,
And they won't let a poor boy down.
Sure as you're born, they bought me a silk suit,
They put luggage in my hand,
And I woke up high over Albuquerque on a jet
to the Promised Land.

Verse 3:

Workin' on a T-bone steak,
I had a party flyin' over to the Golden State,
When the pilot told us in thirteen minutes
He would get us at the Terminal Gate.
Swing low, chariot, come down easy,
Taxi to the Terminal Line;
Cut your engines, and cool your wings,
And let me make it to the telephone.
Los Angeles, give me Norfolk, Virginia,
Tidewater 4-10-0-0,
Tell the folks back home this is the Promised Land
callin' and the poor boy's on the line.

moody blue

Words & Music by Mark James

91

to fig-ure out___ what___ she's all a-bout,___ that she's a wo-man through and through.___
think I know her well, her e-mo-tions re-veal___ she's not the per-son that I thought I knew.___

She's a com-pli-ca-ted la-dy, so co-lor my ba-by

mood-y blue.___ Oh,___ mood-y blue,___ tell me am I

get-tin' through.___ I keep hang-in' on___ try-na

learn the song_but I nev - er do.____ Oh,

mood - y blue,___ tell me who I'm talk - in' to.____

You're like night and day,_ and it's hard____ to say___ which

one is you. _ (2) Well,when Mon - Oh,

D. S. and fade 𝄋

rubberneckin'

Words & Music by Bunny Warren & Dory Jones

Hey, hey, hey, hey, ba - by, that's al - right with me.
We're rub - ber - neck - in' ba - by but that's al - right with me.

Hey, hey, hey, hey, hey. Stop! *Instrumental ad lib.*
Hey, hey, hey, hey, hey.

N.C.

i'm a roustabout

Words & Music by Otis Blackwell & Winfield Scott

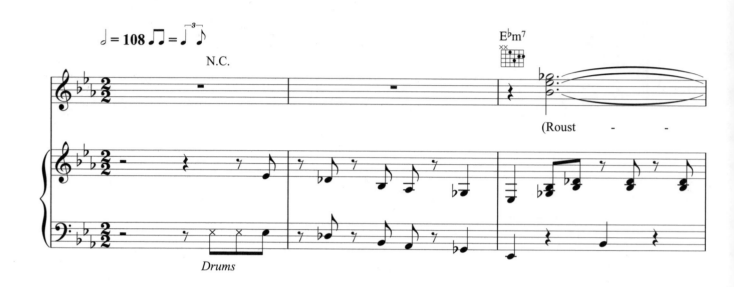

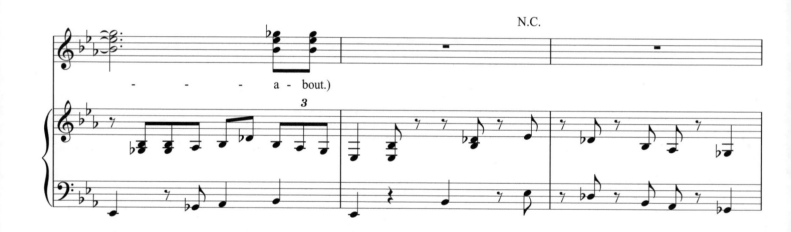